W9-AGM-938

DRAWING
ZENTANGLE®
NATURE

Jane Marbaix and Hannah Geddes

Gareth Stevens
PUBLISHING

Please visit our website, www.garethstevens.com.
For a free color catalog of all our high-quality books,
call toll free 1-800-542-2595 or fax 1-877-542-2596.

Cataloging-in-Publication Data

Names: Marbaix, Jane. | Geddes, Hannah.
Title: Drawing Zentangle® Nature / Jane Marbaix and Hannah Geddes.
Description: New York : Gareth Stevens Publishing, 2020.
| Series: How to draw Zentangle® art | Includes glossary and index.
Identifiers: ISBN 9781538242612 (pbk.) | ISBN 9781538242056 (library bound)
| ISBN 9781538242629 (6 pack)
Subjects: LCSH: Nature in art–Juvenile literature. | Drawing–Technique–Juvenile literature.
| Repetitive patterns (Decorative arts)–Juvenile literature.
Classification: LCC NC825.N34 M373 2019 | DDC 743'.83–dc23

First Edition

Published in 2020 by
Gareth Stevens Publishing
111 East 14th Street, Suite 349
New York, NY 10003

Text, step-outs, and Zentangle Inspired Artworks: Jane Marbaix (zentanglewithjane.me)
Design: Amy McSimpson and Tokiko Morishima
Project management: Frances Evans and Katie Woolley
Outline illustrations: Katy Jackson

The Zentangle® method was created by Rick Roberts and Maria Thomas.
"Zentangle"®, the Zentangle logo, "Anything is possible one stroke at a time", "Bijou",
"Certified Zentangle Teacher", "CZT"®, "Zentangle Apprentice"®, and "Zentomology"
are trademarks, service marks, or certification marks of Rick Roberts, Maria Thomas,
and/or Zentangle Inc.

All the tangles in this book are Zentangle originals created by Rick Roberts and Maria
Thomas, apart from: Barberpole by Suzanne McNeill (blog.suzannemcneill.com);
Heartrope by Bunny Wright, Canada; Cruffle by Sandy Hunter, Texas, USA
(tanglebucket.blogspot.co.uk).

The Zentangle Inspired Artwork on page 19 was created by June Bailey. Dreamweaver
stencils: http://www.woodware.co.uk

Printed in the United States of America

CPSIA compliance information: Batch #CS19GS: For further information contact
Gareth Stevens, New York, New York at 1-800-542-2595.

Contents

What Is Zentangle®?

Zentangle® is a method of creating artwork by drawing simple tangles, or patterns, one line at a time. Zentangle® isn't just about drawing. It focuses the mind, relaxes the body, and builds confidence. With Zentangle®, "anything is possible, one stroke at a time."

Why should I learn Zentangle®?

Zentangle® is great fun to do. The best part is that anyone can do it! It has the happy knack of bringing out the artist in everyone, and this book will help you get started. Remember, the key thing is to take your time. Just go slowly and relax.

What you need to get started!

Pens and Pencils

You can begin making tangles with a pencil for drawing "strings" and for shading. Use a 01 (0.25 mm) black pen for fine lines, and a 08 (0.5 mm) black pen to fill in the darker areas of your pictures.

Paper

Zentangle® art is usually drawn on a square 3.5-inch (9 cm) tile. Good quality artist paper or white card stock is best to use, but you can use any kind of paper. It's a good idea to also have tracing paper on hand, so you can trace images to use as outlines.

Extra Materials

Stencils are fun to use and can be found in art shops and online. Rubber stamps also make great outlines, but you'll need an inkpad to stamp them onto your paper.
To brighten up your creations, you could use pens, pencils, or paints, too.

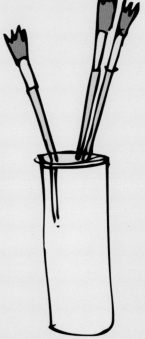

What Are Strings?

The Zentangle® method is different from doodling, as it begins with drawing "strings." These are pencil lines that separate spaces on your paper. The spaces are then filled with tangles. It's as simple as that!

All tangles have names and if you follow the steps, they are easy to do yourself.

A Zentangle® is done on a 3.5-inch (9 cm) square tile. Larger pieces of art are called Zentangle Inspired Art (ZIA).

How to draw strings

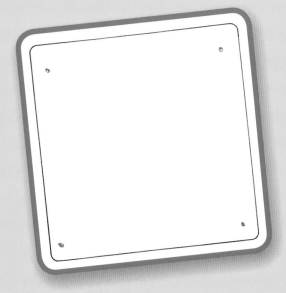

1. Pick up your pencil and draw a dot in each corner of your paper.

2. Join the dots to make a border.

3. Draw two strings as a guide, like this.

4. Start tangling! We've used Crescent Moon (page 9).

5. Next, we've chosen Tipple (page 9).

6. Then, we've used Hollibaugh.

7. We've filled the last space with Chillon.

8. Finally, we've used pencils to decorate the tangles.

Getting Started

Now that you can create strings, let's begin by drawing some simple tangles. These pages show you how to Cubine, Crescent Moon, Tipple, and Zander.

Remember to take your time, and work slowly.

Cubine

1. Begin by creating a grid to fill your space. Next, draw a small square in a corner of one of the squares in your grid.

2. Draw a diagonal line reaching the opposite corner of the square.

3. Continue to fill the large squares on your grid with this pattern.

4. Add shade to your tangle for depth. Fill in the rest of the grid with this pattern.

Crescent Moon

 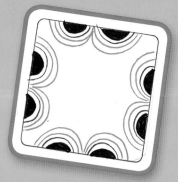 

1. Draw semicircles around the edge of your paper and shade them in.

2. Draw a line around each shape.

3. Then, add some more lines around the shapes.

4. Finally, create a swirling cobweb pattern in the middle.

Tipple

1. Begin by drawing a string of circles touching one another.

2. Draw more circles of different sizes to fill the space.

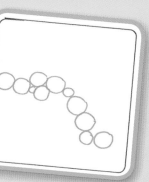

3. Finally, shade in the circles to give them more depth.

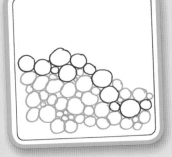

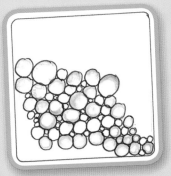

Zander

1. Draw a "band" across your paper. Add pairs of loops around the band, 0.4 inch (1 cm) apart.

2. Next, draw a line through the middle of the band. Don't forget to lift your pencil every so often to add "highlights."

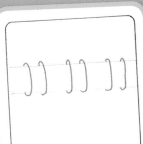

3. Add more lines within the band to fill the space.

4. Finish by adding some shade to your tangle.

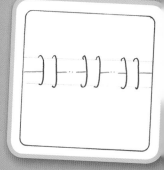

How to Use This Book

Once you can draw some simple tangles, it's time to start experimenting. One way to do this is by creating Zentangle® Inspired Artworks (ZIAs). Throughout this book you'll find lots of great outlines of animals and plants that you can use to create your own ZIAs.

You can also buy stencils from craft stores to create ZIAs. Dreamweaver or Kala Dala stencils are really good to use.

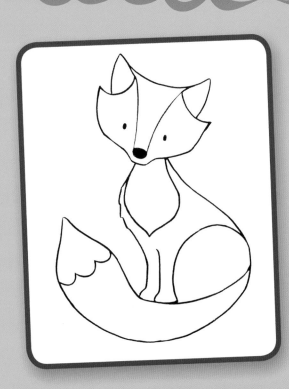

1. Let's start by tracing this fox outline. He's already got strings inside for his face, chest, and the tip of his tail.

2. Draw a different tangle in each string. Pick something bold for his bushy tail.

10

3. Choose some orange pencils or paints to finish off his beautiful coat. Your ZIA is complete!

Keeko
(page 22)

Paradox
(page 28)

Tipple
(page 9)

Zander
(page 9)

Crescent
Moon
(page 9)

You will often come across these words when you tangle:

Shade This means using your pencil to darken areas of your tangle to make it POP.

Highlight These are gaps in the lines you draw in your tangles. They can make your tangle SPARKLE.

Aura If you trace around your tangle, you've added an aura. It can make your tangle come to life!

Trace the outlines onto some clean paper and add some tantalizing tangles!

Poke Leaf

Poke Leaf reminds us of the natural world all around. It's an ideal tangle to decorate this oak leaf shape.

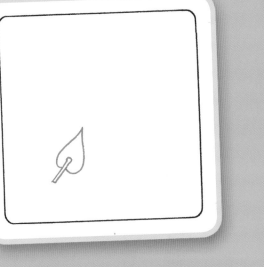

1. Begin by drawing a stalk at the bottom of your paper. Then, draw a raindrop shape around the tip of the stalk.

2. Add more stalk and raindrop shapes to your paper.

3. Then add some shade onto your tangle.

4. Add an "aura" around each leaf for a different look. You can start this tangle anywhere on your paper, as shown here, and see where it takes you!

12

Poke Leaf fills this oak leaf perfectly. Can you trace the outline here to create your own leaf?

Use this outline to trace your own leaf shape!

The following tangles have been used in this project:

POKE LEAF
Crescent Moon (page 9)
Tipple (page 9)
Florz

Try different leaf shapes on your tangle to change the look!

Printemps

Printemps is a circular tangle that looks like lots of spirals joined together! It creates a busy tangle pattern. Why not give it a try?

1. Draw a small circle with a tiny gap, called a "highlight." Add more circles around this first one to make a spiral. You can draw a spiral without a highlight, too.

2. Create more spiral shapes to fill the space.

3. Finally, add a bit of shade to each spiral.

This is a perfect tangle to draw around a poem!

We have used Printemps and other tangles to brighten up this flower. Can you do the same?

Use this outline to trace your own pretty flower shape!

The following tangles have been used in this project:

PRINTEMPS
Tipple (page 9)
Mooka (page 26)
Emingle

Fife

Fife is a tangle that looks tricky, but it's actually quite easy to draw. All you need to do is follow these simple steps.

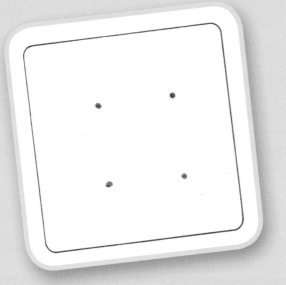

1. Draw four dots on your paper, evenly spaced to create a square shape.

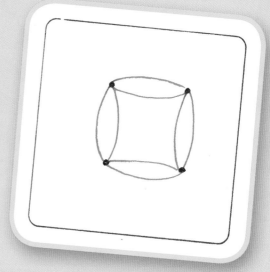

2. Add four oval shapes between the dots to create a rounded square.

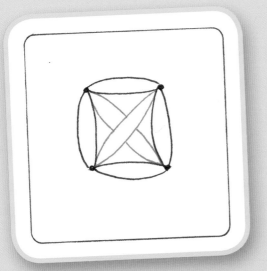

3. Draw an oval shape diagonally from the bottom right-hand corner to the top. Then draw another oval shape in the opposite diagonal direction, going underneath the shape you have just drawn.

4. Add some shade to your tangle for more depth.

You can use Fife and lots of other tangles to decorate this cat. We've tangled our own feline friend here!

The following tangles have been used in this project:

FIFE
Tipple (page 9)
Zander (page 9)
Flux (page 24)
Mooka (page 26)

Use this outline to trace your own curious cat shape!

Remember to take your time with this tangle.

Finery

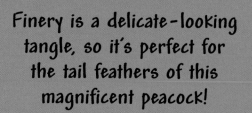

Finery is a delicate-looking tangle, so it's perfect for the tail feathers of this magnificent peacock!

1. Draw pairs of wavy lines to form bands. We have drawn three pairs here.

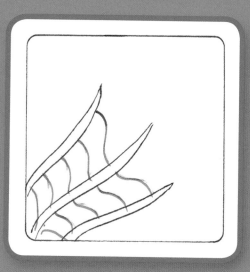

2. Connect these lines with short, wavy diagonal lines.

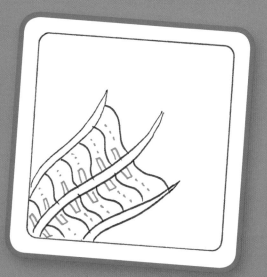

3. Then, add a small rectangle shape and some dots to the spaces between these diagonal lines.

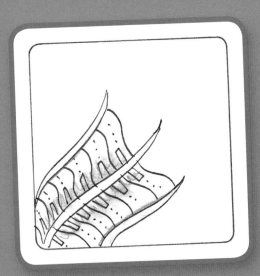

4. Finally, add some shade to create more depth.

You can use Finery and lots of other tangles to decorate your peacock, just like this one!

The following tangles have been used in this project:

FINERY
Mooka (page 26)

You could add a swirl to the end of your bands for a different look.

Use this outline to trace your own proud peacock shape!

Nipa

Have lots of fun creating a tangly texture for this gorgeous seashell.

1. Start by drawing lots of different-sized circles.

2. Draw a wobbly line from the top of the paper to the bottom.

3. Draw more wobbly lines at equal distances apart, but don't draw through the circles.

4. Use a pencil to add some smudges to your circles for extra depth.

We used a black pen to fill in the space around Tipple and Printemps, to draw attention to the structure of the shell.

The following tangles have been used in this project:

NIPA
Tipple (page 9),
Keeko (page 22)
Printemps (page 14)
Zinger
Quipple
Msst
Onamato

Use this outline to trace your own seaside seashell shape!

Now you have a go! Try using a different tangle inside each string.

Keeko

This tangle looks a little bit like feathers, so it's great for this owl! Follow these steps to draw your own Keeko tangle.

1. Create a cross to begin. Draw three vertical lines in the top left square, then three horizontal lines in the top right square. Do the opposite in the squares below.

2. Repeat this pattern to create a band across your paper.

3. Add another row underneath.

4. Finally, shade your tangle to give it more depth.

Easy

Keeko makes lovely fur for animal projects!

Use this outline to trace your own wise owl shape!

The following tangles have been used in this project:

KEEKO
Tipple (page 9)
Cubine (page 8)
Flux (page 24)
Yincut

You can use Keeko and other tangles to decorate your owl, just like this one!

Flux

Flux creates a flowing, leaflike pattern, so it is perfect for this tree picture. Just follow these simple steps!

1. Draw a small, rounded leaf shape at the bottom of your paper.

2. Add another leaf shape; imagine it is growing from a stem.

3. Add more leaves on both sides of the stem. Fill in the gaps between the leaves with Tipple (page 9).

4. Finally, add some shade to complete your tangle.

24

You can change the look of Flux by changing the size and shape of the "leaves"!

The following tangles have been used in this project:

FLUX
Tipple (page 9)
Keeko (page 22)
Zander (page 9)

Use this outline to trace your own terrific tree shape!

We've used Flux, along with other tangles, in the picture above. Trace the outline to create your own tree, then why not add some shades of green?

Mooka

This tangle takes time and practice, so be patient and take it slowly. Follow these steps to give it a try!

1. Draw two "stems" that curve inward, following the direction of the arrows.

2. Then, with one continuous stroke, draw two more stems on your paper.

3. You will end up with this delicate tangle.

4. Finally, add some shade to your tangle for more depth.

Mooka, along with other tangles, is perfect for this horse. Can you tangle your own horse outline?

Use this outline to trace your own majestic horse shape!

The following tangles have been used in this project:

MOOKA
Tipple (page 9)
Printemps (page 14)

You can draw Mooka with "stems" that curve outward, too.

Paradox

Paradox is a mind-bending tangle! Its 3-D pattern does take a bit of practice, though. Let's give it a try!

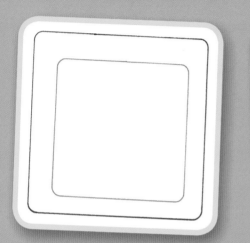

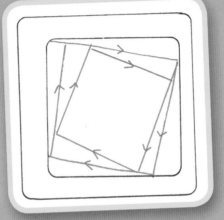

1. Begin by drawing a square.

2. Add a line to the top of your square. Turn your paper 90°, then add another line to the top of your square. Turn again and add a line, and again to add a fourth line. You've made a small square inside your first one. Repeat.

3. Keep adding smaller squares inside one another, turning the paper each time.

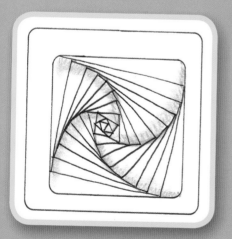

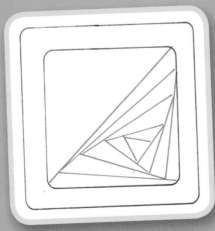

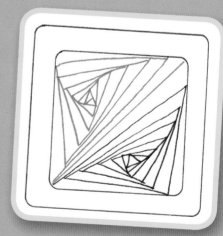

4. You'll end up with this busy-looking tangle! Add some shade to finish it off.

5. Try drawing Paradox inside a triangle for a different look.

Paradox is great for creating "animal stripes" in your pictures. It's perfect for this stripy tiger!

Use this outline to trace your own wild tiger shape!

The following tangles have been used in this project:

PARADOX
Crescent Moon (page 9)
Tipple (page 9)
Keeko (page 22)
Zander (page 9)
Cubine (page 8)

Remember to turn, turn, turn!

Glossary

cobweb   a spiderweb

diagonal   a straight line at an angle

horizontal   a straight line from left to right

outlines   shapes with clear outlines that you can trace through another piece of paper

semicircle   half a circle

spiral   a shape made from a line moving outward in a circular pattern from a central point

stencil   a shape that you can draw around

strings   pencil lines that separate spaces on your paper

tangles   a simple pattern that you repeat to fill a space

vertical   a straight line from top to bottom

ZIA   stands for Zentangle® Inspired Artwork

Further Information

Books

A First Book of Nature by Nicola Davies and Mark Herald (Walker Books, 2014)

Being a Bee by Jinny Johnson and Lucy Davey (Wayland, 2017)

Inspiring Zentangle Projects by Jane Marbaix (Arcturus Publishing, 2016)

Nature Origami (National Trust) by Clover Robin (Nosy Crow, 2018)

Nature's Day by Kay Maguire and Danielle Kroll (Wide Eyed Editions, 2015)

Questions and Answers About Nature (Lift the Flap) by Katie Daynes and Marie-Eve Tremblay (Usborne, 2017)

RSPB Nature: A Seasonal Colouring Book by Flora Waycott (Bloomsbury, 2017)

Tangled Treasures Coloring Book by Jane Monk (Creative Publishing International, 2015)

The Nature Explorer's Scrapbook by Andrea Pinnington and Caz Buckingham (Fine Feather Press, 2016)

Woodland and Forest (DK Children, 2017)

Websites

https://zentangle.com Start by taking a look at the Zentangle® website. There's lots of information on tangles and the story of the founders of this art form.

www.funology.com Have a look at the funology website for craft ideas as well as recipes, trivia, and games.

www.natgeokids.com The National Geographic Kids website is packed with information about animals and amazing places.

www.pinterest.com Look up Zentangle® on Pinterest to see other people's work and ideas. (You will need to be 13 years old to open an account, or explore with a parent or teacher.)

www.metmuseum.org/art/online-features/metkids/Check out the kids' section at the Metropolitan Museum of Art to find a great guide to amazing artwork.

Index